The Absolute Cheapest Way to Start a Doggy Daycare Business

How to easily start a successful doggy daycare business the cheapest and simple way, in the next 2 hours!

Bernard A. Savage

Contents

Chapter 1

The best home-based business……………………… 1

Chapter 2

The easy way to get your business license…..9

Chapter 3

The best way to market your business………..17

Chapter 4

The cheapest way to get customers…………….27

Chapter 5

The easy way to make flyers………………………..55

Chapter 6

Door Hangers the fast, easy way to success…62

Chapter 7

The best way to manage your income…………80

Chapter 1

The best home-based business!

Whether it's a dog or a cat, a pet is part of our family. If that's true, we wouldn't want a family member, home alone eight, ten or twelve each day. That's why people are turning toward the pet daycare business, making it one of the best home-based businesses you can start for under $100.

Why are some people successful in the pet daycare business while others are not? Because a smart professional dog daycare owner researches and plans their business before investing one dime toward his business start-up capital. He sets up a simple business plan and sticks to it, slowly but surely working his way toward success.

Why does a person fail in the pet care industry? People jump into this business thinking, if a friend or neighbor is successful, I can be successful too. I know how to start a pet daycare, I'm a better business person than them, and I will be a success as well.

In the dog daycare business, it takes a lot more than being a good business person. You must know how to promote your business, how to manage your day to day operation, and how to acquire customers, keep customers and us that customer to help you promote your business. When the clients start calling and money begin coming in you must know how to manage that income so you will stay in business for years.

I have always said that your first three years in business is the hardest part. From years of being in the business industry myself, and talking to other successful business owners, we have come up with a simple pet daycare business plan, which will get you clients not only today but for weeks as long as you continue using it.

Did you know that the main reason people lose their business in the first year is because they are unable to target clients. Clients, to a home-based business, are like fuel to a fire. You cannot survive without them. Without customers and knowing how to pay your money out, I guarantee your business will not survive the first year.

What you are holding in your hand is the first step on your road to success. I may not know all the answers but I know how to make money in the pet daycare business and after reading this book, you will to!

The smart business man would spend some time mastering his craft. Your craft is caring for dogs and you master your craft by working with dogs over and over again. You can use this system as a way to promote your future pet daycare business. This is how it works.

I went to a local dog park in my town, to talk to some dog owners and told them about my pet daycare business. After getting their attention, I offered to care for their dog free to show them how happy their pet will be when they use my services. This allowed me improve my skills while promoting my business.

Offering something free is the best way to open the doors in any small home based business. People love free offers! Think about it. How many times have you walked through a supermarket and seen people gather to watch a demonstration, just to receive a free gadget? I know my wife can smell these offers when we walk through the doors. If I lose her, I just look to where people are gathering and she'll show-up 20 minutes later, smiling, with some gadget in her hand.

Watching this gave me an idea. Why don't I offer free services to gather dog owners into my service? Think about it. Would you refuse an offer to watch your dog free of charge?

The benefits for a new pet daycare service are great. For one thing, you get free advertisement. This works 2 ways; word of mouth and reference letters. I also take pictures of dogs playing at my center which I attach to the reference letter and keep them in a folder to show to new customers. Words are one thing but you know what they say! A picture says a thousand words.

Another thing we did was offer the client regular

services once a month at a reduced rate. You might want to go easy when you start, cutting your rates to build up your customers list. Let me put it this way. If a client tells me, "I cannot afford to have their dog care for by a daycare center." I'll counter by saying. "What can you afford to pay?"

We also offer 1 week free for every reference a customer sends us. I remember Alice, a 70 year old woman we made this offer to, telling her women's club about my services and we acquired 12 new customers and Ray, her dog, received 6 months of free daycare service.

In this book, you will learn my top secret system,

which will show you how to use free offers to start this business without investing a dime out of your pocket and turn your business into a six figure income in the next 24 months. To get this system started, you'll only need a pen, some paper, and about 2 hours of your time.

It doesn't matter if you want to just pay your bills doing this business part-time or if you want to earn a full-time $100,000 + yearly income. You have just made the best move you have ever made in your life. Are you ready? Let's make money as a pet daycare business owner.

Chapter 2

The easy way to get your business license:

If you're trying starting a home based pet daycare business in most counties you must have a business license. It is the law. If you try to run a business without a business license, you will be fined or, in some counties, arrested.

Do you need insurance to get a pet daycare business license? If you're operating a pet daycare business in Fayette County, Kentucky, you don't need insurance to get license. Different states and counties have their own laws regarding licenses and insurance. To find out what's needed in your County call the County Clerk's office. They will tell you what you'll need to do.

First, decide what you want to name your business. Look for something snappy and easy to remember. I have put together a few names to give you an idea. You are welcome to use any name but be sure no one else is using the names in your state. Check with the County Clerk's Office.

*Doggy Play Room   * Pet's Care Inn

* Pet Lover Are Us   * Flea Dip Cats & Loving It

*Pet Clips   * Little Rascals

*Your Pet's Play Pen

*Dogs Resort

Some home businesses believe if their company has a professional name, it will help them get more clients. I disagree. It doesn't matter what you call your business. If you follow the plan in this book, your business will be successful.

This is what I did. I wrote down several names for my pet daycare business. After I talked to several friends and asked them what service sounds more professional and which name got their attention.

That's what you're looking for a name that catches the clients' attention.

Once you come up with the name call your local Commissioner of Revenue office, which is located in the County Clerk's office in the county governments building. They will help you get a business license. They'll need to know what business will you be running and your business address. You must live in the county where your pet daycare service is located.

If you go to another county and pick-up customers, you may have to pay a county tax for that area. Once again, contract the County Clerk's office to find out the laws regarding the business.

This is a how it works, if you live in Fayette

County but you start pick-up accounts in Franklin County, 12 miles down the road. Franklin's Commissioner of Revenue office may want their 4.5% annual taxes for you doing business in their county. I know it sucks but it the law. I would rather pay $30 to $50 per year in county taxes to be fined $300 to $500 for not paying taxes.

Some counties may check the Zoning Department to make sure your residence is zoned for a pet daycare business. I have never heard of a county refusing to give license to a pet daycare service unless you have a fleet of vehicles and a 20 man operation. If that was the case, you wouldn't need this book, you would be writing one.

Will you need a Tax ID Number? I don't think so. If a woman is going to hire you to care for her little Cairn Terrier, I don't think she'll be worry about a Tax ID Number. She'll want you to watch her Cairn Terrier.

Do you have employees or planning on hiring someone in the next few weeks? I wouldn't think about hiring anyone until I have more business than I can handle. Once that happens, I will hire someone part-time. When you're hiring full-time employees, it's time to get your Tax ID Number, Social Security, and Worker's Compensation insurance.

Do I need Worker's Compensation Insurance? If you hire employees, yes. If your employee is bite by a dog or cat, you will need insurance for protection.

"Google" Worker's Compensation Insurance and you will be directed to several sites which will to give you a list of agents in your area.

Do you need liability insurance to start a dog daycare business? In the state of Kentucky, you do not need liability insurance to start or get license for dog daycare service. But I would check my Commissioner of Revenue Office to be on the safe side. If they do request liability insurance, I would work alone until I have the money to get the right insurance.

This is my opinion; if an employee drops a tub of water and breaks his foot, I don't have $2400.00 to give to my employee for doctor bills. It will shut my business down before I get the doors open. Get the insurance and keep it as long as you're in business.

The reason for liability insurance is to protect your business, just in case something, like an employee breaking their foot happens. But that's my opinion. It's left up to you.

Chapter 3

The best way to market your business:

Now you have your business license and insurance, next is the location.

Most small, one person dog daycare businesses don't have an office because you can start a pet daycare business in your home. The only thing you'll need is a phone to take calls, a free room or basement.

If you just start a dog daycare business don't

go out and rent a building with high monthly payment to get started. You need to set up a strict budget and stick to it.

If you have a lot of supplies, all you will need is a spare room, or a basement would be perfect. Some place you can clean out and put down an in-door-out-door carpet. This room or rooms should be clean and smoke free.

It's my opinion that if you are a smoker, doesn't smoke in a confined room with the dogs. Wait until you leave the room. I'm not trying to rag on you if you're a smoker. That's your business. But there are people who don't want their pet coming back home smelling like cigarette smoke. But if you are a smoker, make sure the area where you keep the supplies and dogs is smoke free.

Keep a report on every pet you care for. This will tell you the date of service, what the customer wanted, condition of the pet, what you did, and how much it cost. The customers know their pet. They are the boss, do what they tell you, when they tell you, and you will have a happy client. If a customer requests to walk their pet three times daily, don't try to talk them into a complete doggy

Make over just to run their bill up. Just walk the dog. Be honest, giving them what they pay for, thanking them for the business, and moving on the next job.

You are a professional. Make daily notes on every job. This is very important, which is why I'm saying it again. If you purchase a special dog treat because your client requested it, get two receipts; one for you and one for the customer.

If you see any marks, cuts or bruises on the dog's body, call the owner right away. Take pictures, record the time and date, and anything the owner said and keep it in your files. If you have a witness, get a statement from them about what they seen. Get the statement in writing and put it in your files. When the parent comes to pick-up their pet, have them sign a statement about what you reported and what they said and give them a copy.

Do not tell the owner about your pictures or about the employee's statement. Protect yourself and your business.

If you have a pet that continues to show up with marks, cuts, or bruises keep notes and call the Animal Humane Society. Protect yourself and that animal, let the Humane Society do their job.

You may lose a client but believe me, friend, you could save that pet's life.

Keep the pet's area clean. This is where the clients come in to pick up their babies. It should be cleaned every night and disinfected once a week.

If a pet vomits or uses the bathroom in the area, clean and disinfected right away because other pets will smell it and try to put their mark over it. Plus, it's bad business for a client to walk in and see a pet's mistake on the floor.

You should have an area for cleaning rags. We remove them from the pet's area. Secure them in a bag and later that evening, we double secure them in another bag and remove them from the house. It's safer for the health of you, your family, and the pets.

Get your Pet's Cardiopulmonary Resuscitation or (CPR) certification. Call your local Humane Society. They would be able to tell you how to get the certification free. Once you get the (CPR) certification, frame it and hang it up in the pet's room.

In some counties it's a requirement to have a

(CPR) certification to receive your dog daycare license. It may take 4 to 6 hours of your time but my opinion is it will help you get clients and you need to have your certification.

Keep doggie treats and snacks on hand. Healthy snack works better. Talk with the owner to see what snacks their pets like.

When your client comes to pick-up their pet or you drop the pet off, make sure you thank them for their service. Let them know how much fun you had caring for their pet. Call the pet by his name; please don't say, "I really enjoyed your dog or cat." If his name is Scout, tell them, "I really loved Scout. He really is a sweet-heart." Three days later mail them a thank you letter, letting them know again how much you loved Scout and look forward to doing it again. This simple letter will help your future relationship with the client.

People wonder how we are able to keep clients coming back year after, year, after, year. I'm going to tell you the secret to keeping your clients coming back. On every holiday, mail them a card thanking them for their business. On Christmas, we send our clients a box of Christmas Cookies and a box of their pet's favored treat. If we do that, 90% of our clients always come back.

Sounds simple, doesn't it? Well, try it, my friend! It's worked for me and it will work for you.

One of the most important things to remember when the customers start using your service: Always ask them how they heard about your service. This simple marketing tool will help you use your advertising dollars more wisely.

You should also ask them who care for their pet before and why they aren't still care for their pet. Use any valuable information gathered as a way of promoting your business.

Chapter 4

The cheapest way to get customers:

Like gas to a fire, clients are the life force to any business. Customers pay your bills, put gas in your car, feed you, and keep your business operating in a professional way. Just like any business, you need customers to stay in business. Not one or two but a steady stream of clients.

Let me tell you how I got my first 10 clients with 25 flyers. In Lexington, Masterson Station Park has a dog park where all the dogs go and play. I walked the area, talking to the dog owners, handing out flyers. I notice that a completely different group of people came to the parks on weekend because these were the working families. This was our main target.

I would introduce myself asking them, "Who care for your pet when you're away?" Sometimes, I would talk to several people at the same time. Once we started talking, and have feedback, I would offer my daycare services free for 1 week.

If the customer was using another pet daycare service, I would ask them the following questions:

The name of the service:

Were they happy with the service?

If not, why not?

What can they do to improve their service?

What attacked you to the service?

How did you find out about the service?

How much do they charge?

    Do not put another pet daycare business down. This is unprofessional. It is wrong and bad business. If the customers have something bad to say about another listen and take notes but do not voice an opinion. If you don't have something nice to say about another man's business, don't say anything.

Keep notes on the customer's replies and use this information to market and improve your dog daycare business. Always ask them how they heard about the pet daycare service. This simple marketing tool will help you advert more wisely.

This is valuable information, if you are new to the business, lets you know what has made the other business successful and what works in that area.

A good marketing system is using what other people say to market your business. If I talk with 18 clients who say, "We love Blue Sky Pet's Daycare! They brush my dog's teeth for free," when I talk with my next customers, I will say, "At my place we brush your pet's teeth free." This is one of the oldest, most successful tricks in the business. Find out what the other guy is doing and do it better.

That's why we ask the clients about their dog care. If a client looking for another pet daycare, we ask them. "Weren't you happy with the service of Blue Sky Pet's Daycare? I heard they have a good system."

"No, the place was dirty and it smelled like dog poop every time I walked in."

"Susan, at our pet daycare, we try to keep

the place cleans for the health of you and your pet. We have employees who' clean up and disinfect mistakes as soon as it happens."

Talk to your customers, learn what they like and dislike about the other pet daycare services, then think of how you can better your service.

Pricing your service is also very simple, if you know what to do. Talk to your customers to find out how much the other services are charging. You can also call them or walk-in and ask. We don't believe in low bidding just to get clients. But we believe in a fair bid. If the going rate is $45 to $70 a week, I would charge $60 for my service.

We offer 1 week Free to anyone who signs up for monthly service. Free is one of the strongest words in the business industry. By offering something for free it opens the door just wide enough to get your feet in, even in the hardest markets.

Taking pictures of your pet daycare area and inviting the owners over for a walk through, gives you the opportunity to get to know the client and the pet. We also prepare a snack for the pet, to show the client what their pet would be eating under our care.

If you don't have any money to start your pet daycare business there's other ways that you can get clients within the next 7 days, using the people you know. This way is simple but very successful and people are using it every day.

Sit down and make a list of everyone you know. Make list family members, friends, neighbors, and their landlords or property managers, and acquaintances. You need their addresses and phone numbers.

Start with your family and friends. You can call them, but I think it's better to talk with them face-to-face. Let everyone know you are starting a pet daycare business and ask for help.

What you are trying to do is get a list of pet owners who would like a free pet care service. Pet owner's needs pet care. People just don't have the time, and it's better to hire someone you know that to bring a stranger into your home to care for your pet.

Talk with your spouse; make a list of all the people she knows. People she works with, church members, gym members, and acquaintances.

Acquaintances are people like your doctor, dentist, mailman, landlords and veterinarian. Talk with your children and get the names of their teachers, their best friends' parents, and school bus driver.

You can keep your list growing by asking family, friends, neighbors, and acquaintances to fill-out a list of everyone they know. Let people know that this information is very important and you'll need it as soon as possible.

What I did was call everyone on my list and invited them to a chili dinner. Who doesn't love chili? It's cheap to make and most people will not turn down a free meal. Over 35 people showed up, I told them about my pet daycare business and asked them to write down every pet owner they knew before leaving my home. To my amazement, I picked up 5 customers and a list of 92 pet owners.

I also made a special offer to the people I invited to the chili dinner. If anyone on their list used my service, we would give their pet free for three days.

One guy called his veterinarian who had several clients who owned dogs or cats in need of regular daycare services. The next day, I sat down with the veterinarian and we came up with a fair agreement. I would take care of all his customers and groom his dogs for free. He was the owner of four 6 month old Saint Bernard puppies. I also agreed to buy all my shampoo and flea dip from him to use on his customer's pet.

Let's look at it this way. My investment was $35.00 for the business license, and $60.00 for the chili. This one account turns out to be a $10,000 per year account. Not bad, not bad at all.

For the next 2 weeks, I worked the list, mailing out letters and phone calls, pulling in 12 more clients.

10 customers

New Customers $25 per day

Estimate 1st Weeks Income $1250

Every client is a walking advertisement. Your clients can get you customers quicker than any TV or radio advertisement. Once I had established myself, I made the following offer to my customers; 1 free week for every new customer they send me. That word "Free" worked its magic, pulling in 5 new customers in 2 weeks.

You can use this same offer to turn your pet daycare business into a 6 figure yearly income. It works better for people with big a family or a lot of friends. The more people they know the longer your mailing list. The longer your mailing list the more customers you will get.

If you are trying to start the pet daycare business but you have no start-up money and have bad credit, then you must put together a money making plan that will help you to get your business started without investing any money. You can start a pet daycare business without money, but it will require some work and the help of friends and family.

Offer to pay cash for each new customer that is sent to you by friends, neighbors, and family. You should use a cash offer that will not take too much of your profit. A good amount to offer is $20 per new customer, if profits from the business allow. Explain that as soon as the customer pays you, you will pay for the referral.

Make a flier on your computer and print out copies to hand out to people in the neighborhood, friends, family members and anyone you meet who expresses an interest in your business.

I offered free grooming services or $20 to my friends, neighbors or family for every new customer referred to me. I made the same offer to new customers, free services or 50% off the next two weeks service for every new customer you send.

Rent-A-Center made tons on money using this same system on their rentals. Offering their customers half off their next payment or the next payments free, for every new customer referred to them. Now banks are using it! My bank pays their customer $50.00 for every new account they referred to them. It simple, it is a way to get customers without investing any money and it works.

Get Mother to have Bake Sale:

   People love cookies, cakes, pies, and cupcakes, and are willing to pay a little more money for cookies they didn't have to make themselves. Because cupcakes are inexpensive, easy, and quick to make, they are an ideal business start-up project. Get together with your friends, family members, and neighbors to hold a pet grooming business fundraiser. You might be surprised by how much money you can earn for your business start-up capital. I have a friend who started an office cleaning business using this idea three years ago and is now earning over $300,000.00 a year.

You need to set the time and date for your fundraiser. Because cupcakes are good if the weather is cold or hot, they can be held at any time of year, and mother and grandmother needs to know ahead of time to give them enough time to make their worlds famous chocolate chip cookies.

My mother and girlfriend had spent three days baking cookies for my pet daycare fundraiser. We went to the Dollar Tree and purchased several boxes of freezer bags and I stuffed them with cookies. I talked to the manager of a local Kroger and asked him about setting up on the sidewalk out-side the entrance. He asked what it was for and I said, "A fundraiser." I offered him a dozen of my mother's world-famous chocolate chip cookies, and with a smile, he agreed.

Set your prices. The last time we paid for a dozen of cookies from Sam's Club it cost me $6.50, we offer a dozen home-made cookies for $10.00 and sold out. We earning over $800.00 dollars in 4 hours. We all agreed with splitting up the money $150.00 for my mother, $150.00 for my girlfriend, and $500.00 for my pet grooming business. That was how a broke man started his pet daycare service.

Have your friends go through their homes looking for items you can sell at yard sales, through online classified ads Craigslist or eBay. Have a yard sale to get rid of large and bulky items you can't ship. Place free ads on Craigslist or hang-up signs to promote your yard sale.

The best way to start a pet daycare business without any money is to get into your car or truck, put the tools in the back, and drive through neighborhoods and look for houses with dog doors or sign of pets. Go to the door, introduce yourself, and make them an offer to keep their pet for free. Also, give them a price for regular services. Keep your rates low, but fair.

I know services that have used this little money making trick several times over the years. The first time I used it, I earned $150.00 dollars in five hours. The second time, $200.00 dollars in five hours and I still have those customers today.

Ask current clients if you can post a company sign in their yard as you take care of their pet, and see if they will allow you to leave it there for a couple days after you complete the job. Offer a promotional discount to those who allow you to advertise your business this way.

If you do a great job with each and every client, they will recommend you to their friends. Make follow-up calls after a job is completed to see that clients are satisfied with your work. Ask them to refer you to friends and family and ask them to write a short letter talking about your services. Take pictures of all dogs you service. This will be used to log your improvement and to show to new customers.

This is another good way to get started in this business with no money, and free advertisement. Let your work talk for you. Do a thorough job and pay close attention to details. Be meticulous so you do not overlook anything. Make your pet daycare services an art to make all your customers happy.

Let your customers view your place before they leave. If there is anything they are not happy with, try to correct it. If you cannot, offer to give their next week free. The important parts of this business are to make sure your customer pleased with your service.

How about a local fish fry? If you like to fish or have a friend who a fisherman, people love fried fish. You could charge up to $7.00 for a fish sandwich and $10.00 for a plate. You can get some baked beans and coleslaw for the plate or meal.

I had a cousin who opened a Lawn Care Service; he didn't have any money, car, lawn mower, trimmer, or blower. After selling fish every Friday and Saturday for 2 months he was able to get all the equipment needed to start his business.

Chili worked for me. On a cool fall weekend on Saturday and Sunday after church there's nothing better than a hot bowl of chili or soup.

The best way to advertise your chili, fish fry, or

any food sale is churches and word of mouth. Have some flyers made up with "Fish Fry" or "Hot Chili" at the top with your name, phone number, and times and dates on the bottom. Passing out the flyers in your neighborhood or placing those on cars at local churches should get a lot of business. If you ask a week or two before the date of the sale, some churches may announce your sale to their members. This will work better if you offer to donate 10 to 15% of the profits to the church.

Make a list of everyone you know, and tell them about your food sale. Don't forget to tell them that you're trying to earn money to start-up a pet daycare business. Most true friends will want to help you so the more people who knows what you are trying to do, the better for your business.

HOT CHILI SALE

FOR DOG DAYCARE BUSINESS

START-UP CAPITAL

PLEASE HELP!

438 RACE STREE

1 PM-TO-7PM

FIRDAY, SATURDAY, & SUNDAY

DATE:

Vegetable Soup Chicken Noodle Soup (Sale)

FOR DOG DAYCARE BUSINESS

START-UP CAPITAL

PLEASE HELP!

438 RACE STREE

1 PM-TO-7PM

FIRDAY, SATURDAY, & SUNDAY

DATE:

FRIED FISH SALE

FOR DOG DAYCARE BUSINESS

START-UP CAPITAL

PLEASE HELP!

438 RACE STREE

1 PM-TO-7PM

FIRDAY, SATURDAY, & SUNDAY

DATE:

SWEET BAKE GOODS SALE

FOR DOG DAYCARE BUSINESS

START-UP CAPITAL

PLEASE HELP!

438 RACE STREE

1 PM-TO-7PM

FIRDAY, SATURDAY, & SUNDAY

DATE:

Chapter 5

The easy way to make flyer:

We use thicker paper with a glossy finishes. A bright color makes the flyers stand out, getting the customers attention. Decide on a color, preferably something that will stand out so people will remember the flyer. A bright yellow paper with the heading in red has worked for McDonald's for years. That's why they're so successful and with the right heading, like "YOUR FRIST WEEK FREE" will get you a better reply.

Before you have your flyers printed and delivered, are you ready for business? If a client calls you late that afternoon and says, "I need a dog sitter by 7pm tonight" are you ready? Decide on a date for your opening before you send the flyers out.

You can use the open date with a special offer like:

"FIRST WEEK'S SPECIAL

ONE FREE PET BATH &

FLEA DIP IF YOU CALL

BEFORE FRIDAY"

Put the date on the flyer and if you're offering specials for the opening day or for the first week of your opening include this information, as well.

Get your customer's attention with the title and keep it with the body of the letter. How about;

5 DAY FREE FOR MONTHLY CUSTOMERS:

You can have the coupon at the top to grab people's interest.

Add an incentive for keeping the flyer, such as a coupon like ($10.00 Pet Bath Service THIS MONTH ONLY for the first 10 people who call). If you are making this offer, your phone ring offs the hook. I have had customers calling me at 5 o'clock in the morning, wanting to know if the offer still good.

This is how it works. The customer calls you and you respond to the call as soon as possible. Be on time, do your best job, and when you finish, thank those for the service give and them a price list for weekly, bi-weekly, and hour service. You know your client wants the service for their pet, ask them "What days will you want me to you to care for your pet?" You'll be amazed by how well this works.

According to the Direct Marketing Association, flyers and door hangers response rates are usually between 1 and 2 percent.

This means for every 100 flyers you put out, you may get 1 or 2 replies. If your flyer stands out with an eye catching offer that gets your customer's attention. But you may see an increase by adding;

Call a Now Gets Free Flea Dips

Pet care Free

No Obligation!

The flyers' response jumped to 4 to 6 percent. Six customers call for the Free Pet-Care, or:

FRIST WEEKS FREE, THIS MONTH

ONLY for the first

10 people who call!

Fifteen customers responded, but out of the 15, 7 want regular weekly baths of $20.00 per day. Now you are making $140.00 a day or $700.00 a week.

If you follow-up the next week by passing out more flyers and pick-up six more customers, you are making $260.00 a day, $1,300.00 a month.

But to get my phone ringing faster, I added this: (This offer is only available to the first 20 Customers, please be the first to call your number. This works, trust me! You'll have so many clients you'll be smiling, from ear to ear, all the way to the bank.

This simple little technique will give you all the business you need.

What do you do when the phone starts ringing? Give the offer to everyone who calls. I do not care if they are number 30. If it is possible for you to care for their pet, do the best job to make that client happy.

I know what you're thinking. If I make this offer, I'm going to get ripped off. No, not really because getting customers is a numbers game. If you get one regular customer out of every three calls you are getting an amazing response. The truth is that most people will not rip you off.

Chapter 6

Door Hangers the fast, easy way to success:

Door hangers are rectangular in shape and are longer than they are wide. They have a circular hole near the top to slide them and hook over the doorknob. Each door hanger contains a message for the customer, with information about your service. This message can be a special offer for services in their neighborhood.

Like postcards, door hangers are cheaper to print than flyers but have the same response. You can have 3 door hangers printed up on one 8.5" by 11" sheet of paper. If you print up 100 flyers you will get

300 door hangers for the same cost. If you printing up 100 flyers, you can print 400 post-cards for the same price. Remember, getting accounts or customers is a numbers game.

If you want to start earning $2000 to $3000, put out 600 door hangers in a chosen area once a week for the next 8 weeks. Your response will be amazing. Cutting your gas rate down, raising your profits rate, and putting more money in your pockets.

We put an eye-catching and dramatic color photo of dogs playing. We found this will get most customers to at least read the body of the message.

If you own a computer or a friend has a computer, you can make your own door hangers from home. This is what I do.

Pull-up "all programs" and go under a word processing program such as Microsoft Office, Microsoft Word, or Open Office Writer. Next, go under the format tab and select columns. Choose a minimum of three columns and click "ok".

Switch page layout to land-scape by clicking on

the file and selecting "page setup". Choose landscape and "ok".

Now you can start designing your door hanger flyers. You will be able to fit three on a page, one per column. Make sure to include an eye catching title. This should be the first thing your customers see.

Once you have printed out your first copies, ask neighbors for their opinions. Ask them for any suggestions on how to improve your flyer or something that may make them respond to the ad.

You're first printing for the pet daycare service

is a test printing and should be small, 300 or 600. Hand these out and record your response rate by keeping track of the calls. You may decide to do this with a special offer you only advertise on your flyers.

You can adjust the layout and copy of your flyers depending on how well they are received. But I would test this letter every 2 weeks for 6 weeks in the same area before I make any changes.

If you are offering free pick-up and delivery, this will also help the replies. I would stay within 3 miles of my home. Once you start growing, you can put out door hangers in other areas of town.

We put out a ton of flyers and door hangers each week. The best way to do it is to hire a couple kids and pay them by the flyer. Paying them 5 cents per flier and it makes them work faster.

We have also used the area paperboy, asking him to include our flyer in his distribution along with newspaper. They have fixed rates for this service.

On the next pages, you will find some flyers used by other successful pet daycare services. You are welcome to try them or make up your own. They have worked for me so maybe they'll work for you

BUSINESS NAME  PHONE

Don't let your love one spend another day

Alone while you're away!

At our place they can play until

You come home!

We'll provide peace of mind while you're away.

Call Now 1st Week Service Free

Full Day Service Only

$25.00

COMPANY NAME  PHONE

Looking for someone to love your pet while you're away?

We'll provide peace of mind while you're away.

At our place they can play until

You come home!

Call Now 1st Week Service Free

Full Day Service Only

$25.00

COMPANY  Phone

Keeping your best friend happy is like a walk in the park.

We'll provide peace of mind while you're away.

At our place they can play until

You come home!

Call Now 1st Week Service Free

Full Day Service Only

$25.00

Company   Phone

We'll provide peace of mind while you're away.

We give in home care. Your pet will remain at his home or he can come and play in our home with new friends.

At our place they can play until

You come home!

Call Now 1st Week Service Free

Full Day Service Only

$25.00

Company  Phone

Are you working long hours? Do you have a pet? Call us today. Call us today.

We provide in-home care and exercise for your beloved little friend!

We'll provide peace of mind while you're away.

At our place they can play until

You come home!

Call Now 1st Week Service Free

Full Day Service Only

$25.00

Company  Phone

Basic service includes a half hour visit to hour home when you are away. Your visit will include feeding, walking, playing, any necessary medications, and cleanup of any accidents!

We'll provide peace of mind while you're away.

At our place they can play until

You come home!

Call Now 1st Week Service Free

Full Day Service Only

$25.00

Company  Phone

We offers a professional, experience, reliable and dependable dog walking and pet sitting service tailored to meet the needs of you and your furry little friends.

We'll provide peace of mind while you're away.

At our place they can play until

You come home!

Call Now 1st Week Service Free

Full Day Service Only

$25.00

Company   Phone

Is your pet locked up in a cage all day while you are always? Wouldn't you feel better if your pet was running and playing while you're always?

We'll provide peace of mind while you're away.

At our place they can play until

You come home!

Call Now 1st Week Service Free

Full Day Service Only

$25.00

Company   Phone

Did you know if your pet is destroying area in your home it could mean they're not getting enough exercises? Did you know if your dog is put on an exercise program it could stop some or all their bad habits? We'll provide peace of mind while you're away.

At our place they can play until

You come home!

Call Now 1st Week Service Free

Full Day Service Only

$25.00

Company  Phone

Are you tired of rushing home at lunch or right after work? Have your professional pet sitter come instead! We can give them that much needed potty break, with exercise to keep them healthy and happy. Giving you peace of mind while you're away.

At our place they can play until

You come home!

Call Now 1st Week Service Free

Full Day Service Only

$25.00

Company  Phone

Pet daycare will make sure that your dog gets walked, jogged, or make sure they get plenty of exercise when our professional pet sitters come to visit them. This is very important for your dogs which are included in all our pet visit services. We'll provide peace of mind while you're away.

At our place they can play until

You come home!

Call Now 1st Week Service Free

Full Day Service Only

$25.00

Company   Phone

Out pet sitting service allows your pet to remain in familiar surroundings while you're away on business or vacation with as little disruption as possible in daily routines. Not only is your pet walked, loved and taken care of, but the house is looked after as well, possibly deterring any unwanted visitors.

At our place they can play until

You come home!

Call Now 1st Week Service Free

Full Day Service Only

$25.00

Chapter 7

The best way to manage your income:

Warning, warning, warning do! Do try to get too big to fast. This is very, very important. I made that mistake once in this business, using the multi-mailing, and new accounts ringing the phone off the hook. The only thing I saw was dollars. I was too much into making money and was not thinking about running my business. I ended in trouble with the IRS and almost lost everything.

This is a business. When money coming in hand over fist we make the mistake of thinking "I am going enjoy myself, going out purchasing a new car and hiring 10 employees." And the next thing you know, reality hits and you are in trouble.

My simple bookkeeping system which has worked for me for years, is called the 1/4 payroll system. This way everyone is paid. This is how it works. My base rate for daycare service is $20.00 per pet. For every pet I keep, I pay myself $5.00. I pay my company $5.00 and I pay my employees $5.00 and $5.00 goes in an emergency account.

But the trick to making this work for your business is to leave the money in its account. The purpose for paying yourself is living, buying your food, paying your bills and surviving. The money you pay into your business is for equipment, advertising, and gas. This money keeps your business going year after year. The money for employees can be used in two different ways. If you have an employee, it his pay. If not you build up that account for when you do hire someone.

On the business income, use it for mainly advertising in your first year. I would not buy any new equipment because you are trying to build your business account up for the following season. If you do not have start-up equipment and tools and cannot borrow them, I would check yard sales and flea markets. Someone always has tools for sell. Remember, we are trying to build a business, not to go down the first year.

On employee income, I would not hire any employees unless I reach a point where it is impossible for me to handle the work and I would hire only part-time employees.

If you make it through the first year and do not have to hire any employees, that is great. But if you follow the steps in this book, one will need help. Every day you keep a pet take out your employee payroll and one must manage one's money carefully.

At the end of the year, the money is counted to make sure it is balanced with the books. If your income taxes are paid quarterly, you take that money out of your business account. If you are paying it yearly, you would send your money in

February after your working year, taking the money from your business account. The balance in the business account is put into savings for start-up capital for the following year.

If you have employees, you are stepping on bookkeeper grounds. Finding a good, dependable, low-cost bookkeeper is the way to go. They will handle your employee, business, and personal taxes. If you don't need an employee, save your money for the next year.

Almost 98% of the businesses that go under are run by people who do not plan ahead. They will work hard earning $300 and go out and blow the money in a few days. You earned the money, I cannot tell you what to do with it. But if you want to stay in the pet daycare business and earn a good income, follow my system.

Good luck my friend.

Made in the USA
Columbia, SC
05 November 2023